Lighthouses

Also by Allison McVety

Miming Happiness
The Night Trotsky Came to Stay

Acknowledgements

Thanks are due to the editors of *Ambit*, *The Guardian*, *The Huffington Post*, *Magma*, *Manchester Review*, *New Welsh Review*, *The North*, *Poetry Ireland Review*, *Oxford Poetry*, *POEM Magazine*, *Poetry London*, *Poetry Review*, *The Rialto* and *The SHOp* where some of these poems first appeared. 'Afterwards' and 'The "Stradivarius" Tree' were published in *The Arts of Peace: A Centenary Anthology* (Two Rivers Press), 'Finlandia' in *The Best British Poetry 2013* (Salt Publishing), 'White Jeans' and 'Meeting Mallory' in *The Sheffield Anthology: Poems from the City Imagined* (smith|doorstop), and 'Pandemic: Incidents of Mortality' in *The Hippocrates Prize Anthology 2013* (The Hippocrates Press).

'To the Lighthouse' won the National Poetry competition in 2011.

'Crossings' was written for *Traced in the Shadows: ways of looking at poets*, a photographic exhibition by Derek Adams. 'Lookout' was written during *The Poet's Hour in the Tower: a Poetry Trust initiative for readers at the 2010 Aldeburgh Poetry Festival.*

Thanks are also due to Ian House, Lesley Saunders, Susan Utting and Samantha Wynne-Rhydderch.

Lighthouses
Allison McVety

With very best wish

Alli McVety
23/09/14

smith|doorstop

Published 2014 by
smith|doorstop Books
The Poetry Business
Bank Street Arts
32-40 Bank Street
Sheffield S1 2DS
www.poetrybusiness.co.uk

Copyright © Allison McVety 2014

ISBN 978-1-906613-89-1

Allison McVety hereby asserts her moral right to be identified as the author of this book.

British Library Cataloguing-in-Publication Data.
A catalogue record for this book is available from the British Library.

Typeset by Utter
Printed by Printondemand.com
Cover image: © Anthony Ware
Author photo: Derek Adams

smith|doorstop Books is a member of Inpress, www.inpressbooks.co.uk. Distributed by Central Books Ltd., 99 Wallis Road, London E9 5LN.

The Poetry Business is an Arts Council National Portfolio Organisation

Contents

11	White House
12	To the Lighthouse
14	Hedging
15	Departures
16	Finlandia
18	Morte d'Arthur
19	Light House
20	The Light Fantastic
21	Drowning
22	Last Known Good
23	My mother as the Lovell Telescope
24	Crewe
25	Waking
26	White Jeans
27	Saturdays,
28	Eighteenth
29	Nureyev
30	Levenshulme Semi
31	Semi-detached
32	The Mile Road at Midnight
34	The New Fence
35	From the neck of the bottle I stored in the shed
36	Lido
37	Surgeon-god
38	Lighthouses
39	Falling
40	Honeymoons
41	Mallory
42	Bombazine

43	Handsfree
44	Wounds
45	Landings
46	Tightropes
47	Noise
48	Afterword
49	Night Houses
50	The Wedding Gift
51	Sunday Evenings
52	Philomela
53	Dog
55	The Occupation
56	Afterwards
57	Museum
58	Coattails
59	Residency
60	Crossings
61	The Left-Handed Bride
62	The "Stradivarius" Tree
63	Not Speaking of You
64	Requiem from the steps at Pendlebury Station
65	Ivy
66	Pandemic: Incidents of Mortality
67	Man Engine
68	The English Translation
69	Treasure
70	Lookout
71	Notes

for Alan

She belonged to a different age, but being so entire, so complete, would always stand up on the horizon, stone-white, eminent, like a lighthouse marking some past stage on this adventurous, long, long voyage, this interminable ... this interminable life

– Virginia Woolf

If you're a mother, you are either too present or too absent

– Elizabeth Badinter

White House

Alfred Wallis paints the sea through the houses
so the upstairs are flooded. The road is the same
colour as the sea. All the houses are the colour

of sand except his which is the colour of loss
though the sea seeps in. Scrunched eyes bring
seagulls the colour of loss and their shrieks

are the colour of loss and the sky has strands
of loss streaking across it. Chimneys are the colour
of sea or the colour of sand. Their grates unlit

the stacks mute. They don't shriek of anything.
If they shrieked they'd shriek a tissue of loss
and slur with the winds in the sky. The brother's

house is painted small. It's full of sand and no loss.
This skew a kind of revenge. *You are nothing to me*
he paints *not sea not loss and I have silted up your house.*

If this was my perspective and I was painting you
I'd paint you huge – a house offshore in Cornishware
I'd paint you hooped with sea and loss – the one eye
shrieking like a seagull. The one eye weeping light.

To the Lighthouse

i *The Window*

It was Virginia's charcoaled stare
that put me off: her disappointment
in me, the reader, before I even started.
So I walked in to the exam without her:
without the easel, the skull or the shawl,
the well-turned stocking, Minta's
missing brooch. In the hall I watched
the future show its pulse and all the girls,
the girls who'd read the book, set off
together, lined up at desks and rowing.

ii *Time Passes*

You need a daubière and too much time –
three days' absence from the plot. Rump
bathed overnight in brandy, a stout red
brought back from France. The liquor's
boiled once, added back to beef, calf's foot,
lardons, *les legumes*. For six hours – or more –
it idles. It can't be over-cooked. It will not
spoil. At table, a stream of consciousness
breaks out. And it rains. It rains. If not
the stew what was the woman on about.

iii The Lighthouse

The year I gave the book another go,
[the year my mother died], I learned
everything big happens in parenthesis –
marriage, birth, the War. Poetry. Is it the full
manuscript or just the bits in the middle
that count. Is it the woman at the window,
marking the hours, from cover to cover –
or these few lines: that as she eased out from
the bank and in to the water the brackets
of it opened and closed about her.

Hedging

Even before the beech
knows it is a beech,
before the seed
breathes open

in the soil,
before the radical
eels out of its shell,
it knows the word

leaf. Even as it tilts
its pleated panels
to the sun so it knows
of loss and leaving.

All winter it tends
its copper sheaves,
keeps its dead about it.
From soil to soil

it knows and names them:
leaf and *leaf* and *leaf,*
shields itself against
the freeze.

Yet knowing all of this
and, like us all,
each year the beech hedge
can't defend the heart:

translates from bud
to grieving.

Departures

As the train leaves, the LED wipes out its past,
adjusts the future. From the platform,
an ordered row of terraces is all I see.

Red-brick. But as I walk by, the shuttered
eyes give way to movement – a stream of light.
From the street I hear food making its way

to tables and beyond the doors, hallways
are gridlocked with laptops, homework, shoes –
all parked for supper, the hand-to-hand

of pass-the-parcel meals. The other-room
ranting of the tea-time news is a distant tune
I almost recognise. How small the universe.

The earth sobs at the passing of another train.
At home now the land line stirs – it is a brittle sound –
a thin strained voice in the receiver's ear.

On the table five apples soften in their skins.

Finlandia

What I know about death is Sibelius
on the high-fidelity music centre, dad
listening in the dark, gas off, still
in his wind cheater with corduroy trim;
Sibelius so high it distorts the angles of the day;
Sibelius until the street light's eye
is replaced by a cold sun's watch,
by which time my dad has remade my mother
into a living woman, so that we are
not driving the three hundred miles north –
through a slurry of questions with two dogs,
no answers and the wrong clothes for the weather –
just to be with him, and, my sisters similarly,
are not made small again by her absence –
not lost on a day out in Cleethorpes,
waiting at school gates or serving endless
PG Tips and fig biscuits that no one's
going to touch; no, my dad plays Sibelius
with the windows wide, so unfathomably loud
that the neighbours hear it the length of the street;
unaware of this remaking of the day's events
they don't hammer the walls with their shoes
or come to the door to reason or try even
to blot it out with Nat King Cole,
Deanna Durban or Manuel's *Music of the Mountains*,
instead they listen, mourn in their living rooms,
perhaps with a small port or Mackeson's,
so that Coronation Street, The Bill,
News at Ten, all have this soundtrack
behind them ... and across town

in Arthur Gresty's chapel, my mother
might also feel the thud, her blue lips
warming, parting, and for a moment
breathing again; so what I know is the strength
of my mother's love, the volume of my father's.

Morte d'Arthur

First period after lunch – white cabbage,
indeterminate meat, boiled potatoes –
already tetchy, ready for the off, our feet
thumped the herringbone floors of Lyonnesse
and our oak swords, our desk-lid shields,
slammed into battle with us. We went from rabble
to army in one lesson, from school girls
to the latest-left of all his knights. *Be ye
not afeared,* she shouted and we were fearless,
Let them look, she said of those crowding
in the corridor. We were in full-throttle close-
quarter combat, when the whisper of Arthur's
mortal wound broke through the ranks
and took us dumb. And over our ratchet breath
our spittle, Tennyson: her clear voice began:
'The sequel of to-day unsolders all ...'

※

Tonight, we are in the dark and near the end;
me, Bedivere to you, father, namesake of a king.

Light House

I chose not to tell how one night – with the moon's shallow
breaths passing through a window's open mouth,
the loose mesh of the curtains like a waft
of Yardley's *Freesia* – sitting by my dying father's bed,
he'd let go of my hand – the one he'd held,
as he'd always held it – and put his

to the back of my neck, as though he were touching
my mother's neck – the borderlands of black hair
and faint skin – as though she were there in place of me
and they were whispering through
the slow hours of their marriage – or later –
about some future they were planning.

It was such a light house that evening,
as it shifted on foundations, pulled against the tethers
of the crab apple and the gate.

I felt I knew love, its ability to lift
bricks and mortar and there was an airiness
to those few moments – in which the nets trembled,
the ornaments slid along the high-gloss axis
of the windowsill and the pictures tilted,
settled to new perspectives –

before he released his hand, was disappointed
that my face was not hers – the house setting its full weight
back onto our shoulders – and I said nothing
about it for a decade or more because it was mine
and hers and his to have, but I tell it now,
with a sullen rain anchoring the roof.

The Light Fantastic

They left together on the number 42,
with nothing but the clothes they stood up in,
looking out from the back window and singing,
finally achieving the fairy-tale, Hollywood-ending
we'd watched, me between her legs,
she brushing out my long schoolgirl hair.

It was the locum who first alerted us –
my three sisters and me – to our mother's escape,
when he asked, given our father's health
and slackening mind, whether she might be contacted,
whether she could be recovered – though
be recovered might not have been his exact phrase

but rather something said of Lydia Bennet
all those years ago while dad was taking a bus
to Lowestoft or Stranraer, and we were eating
malt loaf or teacakes or crumpets.
She did this of course, because she was selfless –
she did it to spare him the pain of her death.

How confusing it must have been, then, for him
only a year earlier to have followed the hearse,
sat in sight of the coffin, sang *Be Still, My Soul*
when all the while preferring her alive again,
tripping the light fantastic in the Tower Ballroom, hips
chassé-ing, thumb in the nub of her fancy man's arm.

Drowning

[as with Macalister's boy and the fish
so grief has cut a square into our sides

the shock of our wounds
means it is all we can do
to stare from
our numbed eyes

there's no flex left in our bodies
nor can the warm strobe of the keeper's lamps
save us

and our dazzling skins
– now turquoise
– now lilac
– now gaudy with blood
– now lessening

in the fall from light

in the fall from light]

Last Known Good

LKG is a copy of the most recent working configuration and settings stored in the computer's registry for use in disaster recovery

Come Friday, it's Cluster Services,
and the seventeen delegates on the week-long
'Immersion Training for the Non-Technical
(BeNeLux)' are flagging. Normally, the analogy
of two old duffers sitting at their hearth
(with a detour to translate my colloquial
into Dutch or Flemish) is enough to give them
a gist of server-to-server redundancy, the "heart-beat",
the flip, on failure, from one paired node to its mate.

Normally, it's easy to take them, the old duffers
that is, to the close of their days, surrounded
by hard-storage: a box of certificates,
old rent books, photograph albums, a cabinet
of knick-knacks from 'abroad'. Normally,
we visit Walter and Miriam (or Benôit and Mariët)
the one dozing, chin on his chest, the other
taking up the slack, keeping a tally
of the short-term: warfarin, doctors, *Countdown*,

the bangers and mash (or Stoemp) they enjoyed
for supper, what they'll watch on the box tonight.
Normally, we see Miriam's face pause,
the pulse stalling, with Walter now waking
to the absence of her beat, the fail-over of memory,
this shift of last-known-good from her to him,
But today I can't work with the metaphor,
revert to being English and 'abroad',
repeat myself LOUDER, LOUDER. Louder.

My mother as the Lovell Telescope

I find her tilted, head up
and listening, ear shaped for the universe.

On warm days I climb the frame of her skirts
just to lie again in her deep cupped womb,

skin soothed by the dah-dah-dits of the sun.
On the face of it she's a blank sheet

in wait of sound sifting through a black noise
for white notes, a syllabics of stars.

I feel the murmur in her every move,
learn her workings, her subtle pitch and sway.

Listen to the sky waves, she says, *listen,
to the pain of everything speaking at once.*

Crewe

they all came here to change
hometowns slipped out of
like winter coats
accents thrown off
in favour of lighter ones –

and all the while grit
pearling under the tongue

Waking

Waking at four you feel short-changed –
not enough time to get back off
before the pipes and pump clank on.
Half a field away, fox cubs bark

at their own hunger and a milk float
fumbles down the road. The chair
in the corner's filled out as though
gorged on the air that quilts us.

How good it would be to wake, find
someone sitting there, waiting up
to say, *Don't worry, pet, it's only me.*
A freight train dissects the hour,

tyres slur over next door's gravel drive,
some living creature stirs the outside light.
Nights are full of come and go,
you think, but at 4am it's as though

you've arrived too late for a party –
wine all gone and the record player stopped.

White Jeans

I knew I wanted a pair as soon
as I saw them on my best friend
in the communal changing room
in C&A, her mother saying
they wouldn't last five minutes
but both of us knowing that
jeans like that could last a lifetime
of snogs, summers in St. Ives,
Saturday Night Fever, *Close Encounters*,
An Officer and a Gentleman,
Thin Lizzy at the Apollo, Bon Jovi
at the NEC, Depeche Mode, OMD,
three moves up country
and back again, the kids, the splits,
and yet more snogs, any number
of parachute jumps, a wing walk,
and not forgetting the breakdown
crossing Snake Pass. I wanted
to be the kind of girl to wear them –
just this side of safe, just that side
of racy. I wanted them
like I wanted nothing else.
And my mother knew it too:
that white jeans were just the start of it.

Saturdays,

we spent in Lewis's in regulation length
and appropriate footwear, tending the wide
wooden trays of Old Spice and Aramis, soap sticks
and shaving brushes, strops, the tissue sheaths
of single blades, cut-throats, the weekend packs
of ribbed and smooth held *under counter.*

Euphemism is a language all its own
and we learned its codes: not to meet their eyes
when men come asking, not to smile.
We learned efficiency, to keep our fingers mute,
to be invisible, to spirit tender parcels
into bags through sleights of hand.

Across the aisle the girls pair chiffon scarves
with matching gloves: calf, kid, Whitsun lace.
And we learned the facts of life: that it's not
just in hope of sex that some men carry condoms,
but more in hope of being held; the casual,
the scalding possibility of touch.

Eighteenth

I remember my dad's driver's cap
cornering the walk before he did, how
he leaned in to the wind on a calm day.

One moment, it's birthdays at *Tiffany's*
dancing with boys with razor-cropped hair,
the next, it's my dad in a moonless drop,

a field of silk scumbled with soil, the weave
of his cover into the cloth of the locals',
learning at eighteen, what a man can do,

close-quarter, with hands, wire, blade:
quiet deaths winkled out of skins, the shudder,
the body's warm evacuations. 2ams

and men with cars: Vivas, Cortinas, Jags.
And in the streel of his own shadow,
my dad, sweating a mix of diesel and fear.

I remember my dad's driver's cap
cornering the walk before he did, that
he leaned in to the wind on a calm day.

Nureyev

Too early for the theatre bar, there's Oxford Road,
rain lifting 1980s tannins off the brick.
Passing Albert in his campaign medals hawking
copies of the *FINAL!*, I watch the 46 idle at the lights,
windows chocker-blocked. *The Palace* clock

picks off the minutes but it's still too soon
to take my seat. From a taxi steps a man already dying
(though he doesn't know it yet) and I see him
the blackness of his coat, the pits of his eyes,
everything is grace. I've nothing for him to sign

but he looks, a long clear second, through rain.
I turn and he's gone to leap through windows,
eighteen curtain calls, his body's savage argument
with age, his arteries so fierce with blood
they cannot bear his skin. *ENCORE!*

House lights up I take my programme, leave the gods
and him, fly down the stairs and out the foyer doors –
to catch the last bus home, drop into
an empty seat. And so I understand breath –
how raw it is, how infinite it makes us feel.

Levenshulme Semi

Last night my ghost walked in, done up
to the nines and hungry, could scoff a horse
between two bread vans, shoes in hand
and blisters chilling on tiles. Before you know it
the kettle's on and toast – sardines on toast
at 2am, the smell singeing kitchen air –
and she's mumbling – how there's never
any milk in this house. Or heat. She feels the need
to stick the washer on, has had enough of whites,
wants some colour. My mobile phone, free
suddenly from its trouser pocket, is ringing
and tumbling in the suds. Everything now
is funny and nothing matters much. She parks
her bum on the radiator, winks at me,
humming a tune we neither of us know.

Semi-detached

> *I thought how unpleasant it is to be locked out; and I thought
> how it is worse, perhaps, to be locked in*
>   – Virginia Woolf

what it must be to live
alone in a con-joined house listening
through a dermis of breeze-block
the porous membrane of plaster

what it must be to rest
back against a party wall
the thick pulse of arguments
the guffaw beyond a punch line

to hear life always in extremity and be too far
from sleep to numb the after-pub sex
the telephone's rant
the cistern's roar at a vindaloo

imagine all of it this twinned existence
unabridged unpunctuated
its predictable silence its abstract nouns
its cages and cages of words

The Mile Road at Midnight

Perhaps too many *Boddies*
or a lack of witnesses,
but as one day tilts into the next
so hot rods chase the Mile.

In the crook of the road you see
these lads handbrake-turn
a bridge too frail to take
the freight of wagons-and-drags.

Beyond the brink, a ridge
of semis brace for impact.
Hot-hatch and turbo are part-
exchanged as midlife men

tear back from women they
do not love to wives they do not
know. Yet when the belly
of the Mersey swells to flood,

a few still have a bit of spark
to slalom past the road closed
signs, plot a course just wide
of straight and narrow.

Watch them back-end slide
one final run. So many dreams
are cut-and-shut this way
and the ditch is full of those

who've crashed and burned.
All for the Mile – a stretch of road
that's never measured up.
Tonight one man slows, drops

down the years to make it home,
to close the garage door, ignore
the fridge and go upstairs
to watch a stranger breathing.

The New Fence

All that bloody money and the dog goes under it,
nose grounded on some bloody hare or badger.
And no end of calling will get him back,
no, I'll have to gear-up in wellies, gloves, wade

through the barbed wire fence the bloody neighbours
planted out and left to run. He'll be in
the thick of it, of course, shouldering fox shite,
not a thought for me bogged down in muck,

bitten half to death, the sly lick of nettles
on my skin. Oh no, he's in the zone, wild-eyed
and stupid while I race on to beat him
to the bloody road, one ear out for brakes,

the other for his yelp – snagged, thank god,
on next door's bramble, alive with ticks and seed.

From the neck of the bottle I stored in the shed

and took to the municipal tip
they've crowned: five rats
in their cauls of rapeseed oil.
A last squeeze of the plastic
sees them slip still-born
onto the mesh of the drum,
their now hairless selves
freed from the plagues
of their crimes, the myth
of their collapsible bones.

How many times
I've wanted them dead
but here, from the amber
of an easy meal, each one
a slack child spilling
into the world, a windless
blue-child, I'm caught by
the tender dough of their skins.

Lido

Then rain, a few sharp spots stirring the rim
of the pool, then persistent, then heavy.

The others clear off and I'm left to plough on, stroke
after stroke through a sieve of water, of air.

My usual fifty are long behind me and I've found
a liquid rhythm of cup and crawl.

Tech briefings are missed, lunch, the conference calls,
my phone stacking up voices.

And it rains on, even when day dims to night, time now
fluid. At home they're wondering about tea,

why I'm not back for *The Archers* and *Book at Bedtime*.
They go to Wales without me.

Ten years gone and I'm still turning and swimming,
turning and swimming and the world

is feeling the pulse of my strokes, feeling the pull
of one arm after another, one hand

of water making way for the next and the rain is all there is.

Surgeon-god

Relieved of it all: the eggs' recursive ticks
from sudden spring to fallen fruit, the womb's
unreliable thickening and something else,

that unforeseen cast – its scab and pucker –
on an ovary, a blemish that throws a wider blight
than size accounts. Surgeon-god – you

who lift from the pocket of a woman's flesh
creation's screaming force – tell me no more
about this spoiled harvest souring

in your grave hand; its thousand tiny hearts.

Lighthouses

when you were a tree you were one tree
in a row of trees – a beam of dark light
reaching from a fixed point far across the snow
and when I was a bird I was one bird
in a flock of birds – parcels of night

folding unfolding – I added data to the air
the air was a white noise of many voices
all who looked saw the pulse of my wings
saw the world grown bigger

the trees were lighthouses swallowing the sun
asking the birds to come home and when their leaves arrived
when they spoke they were persuasive –
all calling out to the birds and the birds
were sky-ships answering back

build your nests in the crooks of our arms
sang the trees *let us keep you from hawks and kites*

the air lifted to the swoon of their song
we listed to their flightless words
but we were something more than ourselves
by then and – *no!* – we didn't want to land

Falling

with you it was that first slip
from a Cessna
the pack mooning
into a full-canopy

counting

wanting to go up
do it again

Honeymoons
Dubai

For the first few days, here, in Al Maha,
    we drift from moon to moon; the dipping-pool
        mirrors our every naked move; this duned
            skin of land contoured as the six zebra
                who've joined a native oryx herd. Ridges
            shift, drain from one tipped ripple to the next,
    a sidewinder weaves, slips his mosaic
of tiles into shade. These fluid boundaries –
each unfastening itself from desert tides –
  unsettle us all. A man once grafted
      a border on an *antique land* and split
          nomadic Arab tribes. Zebra can't thrive
      in this unfettered sun. Can we? I'm lifted
by your kiss: the black and white of it.

Mallory
Sheffield

I meet him just the once, on the top tier up in thin air
    above the plains of Tinsley. Steelworks echo the glory days,
        metal merchants pan for scrap. He stands, back to the peak,

while I, breathing my last – or so it feels – feel the burn.
    More scree than garden, vertiginous to a fault, it's good to know
        a man who knows altitude, the regolith that takes you

off your feet. I fetch mugs, a plate of garibaldis, mint cake.
    New to marriage – just three months in – the ring sits awkward
        on my hand. On the north face of Everest, gravity slackens

its grip, but here it has me karabinered to rock, not weathering
    the weather well. He says, *some days you can't tell if summit
        is truth or dream*. Dunking a biscuit in his tea, he adds,

Himalayan poppies would do well up here. Hardy.
    Moon-blue petals as fine as his last unsent letter to Ruth.

Bombazine
San Diego

You sail to me on the late flight from Washington.
    December –
                the last of the pacific fleet drops anchor.
      A blizzard of dress-uniforms blurs the harbour.
You're over Utah as I find the only room in town.
    Holiday Inn –
           an almost-view of the Star of India,
        her bowsprit and shrouds denser than creation –

                                            than time.
This is a place of miracles, and luck, we think, is on our side.

You bear fruit and fresh water from the store.
                           Gentler
    than you've ever been, the sheets are calmed, barely guess
      your weight, though still and without our knowing it,
          another child slips port, sets course away from us.
    Sailors throb with paychecks. Their war on hold.
                                  A wind
  picks up –
         tides change, swab decks. This new moon, dressed
    in her bombazine and jet, is sorry for our loss.

Handsfree
Seattle

    Five thousand miles apart, I guide your Leatherman,
sharper than any knife in the apartment, through
    a chicken. We portion the week into dark
        and light. The oysters, we eat where we stand.
    As we cook, you tell me about the hours spent
in the slack space of files. In a Rubik of flesh-tone
    you've found women; in the buffers and stacks
        the numbers don't add up.
                                  Porn:
the work is meticulously grim. I'm amazed
you still see beauty in skin, in me. Sitting by the phones
    in our kitchens we eat dinner. The skies are binary:
        there's a hunter's moon in yours, while here, the milkman
    delivers daylight to the door. And then you laugh, a sound
        so sure, it lifts the pixels of my neck and collarbone.

Wounds
Johannesburg

I think of you cutting your way
    through townships where
        the exchange rate between dollar
            and breath is fatally skewed.
I think of you calling this morning
    with your once-in-a-blue-moon news
        that an August snow is falling
            on the cars in the compound,
    that razor wire
slices the crystals in two. I think of you too,
    as next door, our neighbour sets light
        to love, his recent past, I watch ash
            fall like snow on the laurel hedge,
    fall on the wounded grass.

Landings
Home

On our anniversary, you drag the sofa-bed
    into the old conservatory. The January moon
        swells to cliché and under a ten-tog duvet
we shiver. Frost plays havoc with the view.
Years slip, sheets cool, the roof weeps and timber withers
    in its frame. We are unhinged, the window slides,
        the stars keep their distance, and we, still lovers
of the moon, cling to landings, wipe the rime.
A mist of words mixes up the messages
    between us. You step outside to clear the glass,
        your uncertain face fills the pane and I see
man and marriage eclipse and pass.
I know how Lovell must have felt on Odyssey:
        the moon quite touchable, pulling steadily away.

Tightropes
Away

We go up the full fifteen years to the roof
    of our marriage, step out, cross the shaft of air.
        Our feet trust the slack, familiar as the lies we've told;
           we can't see rope for pavement. In this groove
        of time we've dropped the pole, thinning our weight
    from one hand to the next. We sway through ups
        and downs, soft footing it, you toeing my heel,
           me towing your lead. Our words string the night,
twisting, fraying, testing goodbyes. At perigee,
    the moon is huge, it has our backs. Everywhere
        civil unrest, battles, land shift and cities rattle
on the news. Traffic, like tracer fire, lights the M3,
but up here we are folding ourselves, our pliable soles.
    Are we ending or beginning? who cares? who knows?

Noise
Burgh Island

And when I wake to the sound of no sound
    I think of you sleeping in metre, stressed,
        un-stressed, the rise and falling of your chest,
the count in your neck. The nests in your lungs

    swell. A woman, who isn't me, is stretched
   along the crescent of your spine. She wears
her face the way mine used to be when we
   were lunatics for love and dreams farfetched.

    I leave the vacuum of my room and head
  for a clear sky's uneven murmurings.
    There are no signals here, no calls, no texts.

We were in orbit once and Jodrell Bank
    was listening. The stars on permanent
repeat are speaking tongues, a pulsar beats.

Afterword
Elsewhere

What I remember is this: your mouth blowing
    wet Os in the mizzled rain of the shower door,
the primary signals of odd socks flagging
    along a washing line. Sometimes, the paddles
of your hands pausing the Finch Road
    to wave me out – a monogrammed hanky
still strung at half-mast from the aerial.

Or you, laid out in six-inches of snow –
    the day-moon haunting the sharp blue –
semaphoring *I love you* up to the window –
    the lawn dotted and dashed with sorry feet.
And once, getting your boxer shorts full
    in the face, a wet slap from a makeshift maiden
that you'd slung across a soggy week in Wales.

Night Houses

and think of us now as we are in winter –
see that when the birds left our leaves left too
negatives of what we were when we were filled –

our blank fields a sea an afterword for what was lost
when the birds set their course – their charts against us
and think of us come only to life as light recedes

the ditching sun with all its warmth behind us –
and we are the night houses – arms and lives outstretched –
our lamp rooms howling with a billion blazing nests

The Wedding Gift

When she was asked what married love was,
just weeks after the day she made her vows,
Agnes was careful to set aside the ceremony
as viewed through the fine-gauge of her veil

tethered at the rim with seed pearls and lace,
the breakfast of braised oysters and galantines,
the soft taste of sleep after a night uncovering
the meanings of her body's quiet nave

and how the extent of his interest had quite
dazzled them both. She thought instead
of the present her parents would give her,
they who had known her best in all the world:

that they could think to take her teeth, replace
them with a set of milky beads and how
she and her husband had lain in their places
in ignorance of this false gift: her blanked

mouth, its vaulted ceilings, and had laughed,
ablaze with their new knowledge, that it was
raw like raspberries bursting against
their cheeks, bold as posset on the tongue,

and that since that first night's grace it had
taken on a foreign taint, that they were never
again so naked together, that married love
was Assam sipped across a grazed porcelain lip.

Sunday Evenings

Beneath an incandescent bulb, obscured by blistered glass,
the worship that is the Sunday bath takes place.

It's here a woman's hair uncoils to the length of a hymn,
the flannel finding things to praise in the basins

and steppes – the *fossa/fossae* – of clavicle and spine.
A pumice stone exfoliates the weekly sin, slides

along a natural nap of follicle and pore, each drop
finding its way to pool in the shallows of the lap.

The brain's a chalice, keeper of exquisite thought,
I hear the trickle of the tap, the pattern in the waterfall.

It's here along a clench of terraces that psalms
are read to monthly blood. And pre-menarche,

we girls look up to votives, our mothers' evensongs
through open panes, the sound of holy water –
                                                                its absolution.

Philomela

I remember you, sister, before we took
to the trees, before wishbone and flight.

Days when you sang to the radio,
sewed the names of boys to your lips –

unable to thread a future without love.
I wish you'd sent word sooner,

filled up the skies with your news. I know
now you couldn't wet wool

for the needle's eye – though still wove
trauma in and out of cloth.

How even-stitched it is given the pattern
of your sufferings, the strands of pain,

the ply of your tale. That I did not see it
coming unpicks my eyes.

Time is what we have now, sister, yes,
time to swallow whole what was done to you.

Dog

Long long after the ships,
settled low in the water,
have pushed off from the wharf,
oars cutting and drawing away,
after the last light of the sun
slinks from the shore and back
to the skyline, and the crowds
withdraw to their cooking pots,
their beds, his is the ear that listens on
to the slush and fall, the call
of the wood still speaking plank
to plank in the night. Caught
on the sea air is the tread
of his master walking the deck
and with nose full of the sweat
and piss that the sea winds land,
dog can't sleep, but wades
and feasts on water, as though
to eat fleet and master home.
His insides empty of brine
and still he drinks through the long
reach of his watch. No one
can bear the rank stale stink
of his misery. The hounds turn
on him and he makes his bed
on the warm shit in the stable yards,
his skin scaly with it, flesh
a feeding ground of open sores.
All forget. All but dog and wife,
with their raw hearts held aloft
as lanterns, forget. Servants
weave their days through
and around each other, the men

that once were boys now hunt
and battle each other and the men
who would be kings fester in the halls.
Only dog, with his occasional
catch of blood on a leeward wind,
knows what's what through
the aching years of war. And time
piles on, and he rots from the inside
out and is made ancient, before the scent
of a fast boat and a man disguised
as the sun slinks back into port.
The man passes through the yard
and dog's muscle and bone,
the block and tackle of his frame,
are too far gone to hoist him up,
but he is warmed by proximity
and his tail throbs and his ears
flatten and his master weeps
to have the pup he bred returned,
the years unmade, the roll-call
of dead pulled from the swords
and spears they've met, the nebs
of their own weapons undipped,
the years unmade, to know this dog
tracking the woods as they
give chase, hunt, lie under a fat sun
and by a full river: *what a dog you
must have been*. And after man is gone,
gone to master his house once more,
dog's heart surges on a turn of the tide,
and his ribs ease like the ribs of a ship
and he is gone, gone to the sea.

The Occupation

The waiting room is filled with women
and their luminous skulls. On the table,
The Guardian, folded at five faces shining
out like naked bulbs.
                        In their sinning skins –
their silk camisoles and under slips –
they glow. For them the cost of love
is shears, and after shears – across the scrub
circumference – a cut-throat razor.
Their eyes hold a dimmed after-light
as though they've flared, burned, blown
too soon.
              The women in the room shift,
uneasy in their chairs and gowns, know
sin and cell make convicts of us all.

Afterwards

All men grew *Peace*, but none so well as you,
a silver cup from the local show
as proof of your endeavours.
I have all your garden stuff, you know,
daisy grubber, hoe, the half-moon edging tool
that still looks happy as it works.

The antiquated kit: the brass pump for roses,
your billhook. Mid cut, your rotor mower
takes 40-winks under the cover of the plum,
next to your enamel mug –
the brews that got you through the worst of it.

And always your lads returned,
eyes wide, still in battledress, still baffled
by the permanence of death. Standing,
open-wounded, blood-blackened,
by the new fence and looking to you for orders.

I saw them crowded in your eyes –
how the western desert scorches, desiccates
the flesh. And so I keep the shed door
open to watch you as you graft.
You, Dad, in your element, lost to
thingummies, seed catalogues, doings, string.

Museum

a small place
as though war is a small thing
it makes you want to shout –
something useful – *Look out!*
as though a man
might hear

Coattails

Girl falls from a rooftop looking for comet, New York Times
Amy Hopkins, 19th May 1910

When I fall, I fall big-time and not for the boys either.
It's for you. You who've kept your promise
across the centuries tonight come close enough
for me to grab your coattails and fly.
Leave the charlatans to their cure-pills,
leave the papers to their harbingers and doomsdays.
How can I, at a time like this, be anything
if not alive? I think starlight must taste like snow.
The universe leans in as we pass where you
have been: a beam of gas and dust, a trail
of far-off news and magic. So when I fall,
when I actually fall, I'm looking at you.
The glass roof of the airshaft shatters in welcome.
I have a glittering tail; I am a gift for Brooklyn.

Residency
Found hiding in Crypt of Westminster Hall, 1911 Census
Emily Wilding Davison

I dare not sleep a wink, not now
I'm down in the chapel.
Who could, on a night like this?

Here, in St Mary Undercroft, my breath butted
against Adam's ribs, when overhead
there are whispers in the galleries,
the stampede of houses to the whip.
It's a place of repeats, patterns meted out,
deals mitred into corners.

When they're gone to their beds,
when the last keys have turned in their locks,
I'll leave my hidey-hole for bosses
and hammerbeam, a Jonah's whale of stone.

This night is a line in the records, indelible.
In this place of lawmakers, I am resident.
Behold my house, I'll say, its majesty.
Look at its ogees, its reredos.

Tormentors are at their saints again with fire:
would you look at the blood,
look how the glass has been stained.

Crossings
Ned Parfett, 1912

Not in the photograph but later, the newsboy
will put down the iceberg; the ship breaks up
and all the lost souls will rivet the sea.
The strings of the orchestra will slip their tunes,
the wind section will loosen its last breaths
on the slide of the deck. Not in the photograph
but later, he'll rise from a chill bed, wet with sleep,
shave his newly-conscripted growth, cross
Cockspur – the no-man's-land of six short years –
toward the broad kerb of armistice. Not
in the photograph, but later and two weeks
shy of peace, he'll stumble in the gutter of a shell.
And in the photograph, there's something
in his look-out stare that says he sees what's coming:
the crossing to France, the read-all-about-it headlines –
monstrous numbers looming in the night.

The Left-Handed Bride
1913 Sophie, Duchess von Hohenberg,
wife of Franz, Archduke Ferdinand

that I was so called because my right hand was not worthy of his
that our wedding was as gentian to the Hapsburg lip
that nevertheless he gave up all but the present for love of me
that we are guests, against protocol, of the English crown

that we are come to Windsor in our fourteenth year, ivory, I'm told
that the beech and oaks drop their canopies for us
that confetti is a bronze and golden rain

that laughter here has no sharp edges
that the eyes of the ballroom don't lower as we dance by
that when the men go hunting the skies blacken with flight

that 1700 pheasant were shot yesterday, a 1000 today
that the royal kitchens close their doors on anymore game

that birds hang like morning coats in the castle yards

The "Stradivarius" Tree

*Put your finger on one ring – that is the British Army
going over the top at Ypres*
— Lorenzo Pellegrini, Tree Picker

Only Mr Pellegrini calls me this, only he knows
that what happened that day is an ache in my grain,
that it gave me my key: the long twisted Cs

and high Cs of the whistle blowing them over,
the blast that made a liquid earth, the after-shock
that fled as a wave to the borders of lands,

to this forest and soaked my feet with knowing,
made of me a dark house. With those notes
of mass felling setting the tone for a century

I drew my rings close like a great coat, grew
through it all – height was the only distance
I could put between soil and crown. Lorenzo

would say that fewer branches make for cleaner
sound, but I ask you, what room was there
for tributaries, for light? War plays out its motif

year on year. The decades dry my heart, my wood
fills with a slow sorrow for the numbers. A great
instrument, like a good spruce, Lorenzo would say,

keeps its grief closed, works on it, lets it thicken
to something worth the listening. And its voice,
its voice will drop you where you stand.

Not Speaking of You
> *Tragedies come in the hungry hours*
>   The Voyage Out, Virginia Woolf, 1915

I spend the summer in the cradle of a boat
the sky and sea the kind of black that Manet understood
the reds and blues the yellows obscured by crayon

in this little skiff I have no compass and all the stars
are closed for any business with the living
ink spills across the words I could have written for you

the months drag their nets behind them
a brimming catch that can't be landed
I dip my fingers into water to grab at language
though the thought alone of speech is blinding

on the turn of this night is another where my sail fills with air
the moon writes its signature on blue-white waves and there Godrevey
her intermittent calls break silence not repulsing
but reaching out across the black to speak of you to me

Requiem from the steps at Pendlebury Station
... and suddenly I knew what I had to paint
– LS Lowry 1916

and there was a sea inland – stretching to the hills –
a white water – echoed in the garb of clouds –
and the beacons of chimneys turned their lenses

on the sky – smirring it with black – and a swell of workers
swam to the call of the whistle and the mill was a red house
and the roofs were slate – jagging out at the crowds –

like scuppering rocks – and the people wore lifejackets
in big colours – refusing to drown – and clung to their streets
like Russians – like poets – in their fine coats – their unbroken lines

Ivy
Helen Thomas, 1917

Fair-dos to stick it out through frost
and manic winter. Fussy, some might say:
all umbel and pedicel, all frap and cling.

Others will tell you she stifled him
with her cordiform throttle, her petiole
grasp, with her cat's cradle cage.

But I say that once the elm was dead,
and the bole had rotted down to loam,
she stood on fifty years

echoing his shape, transparently
speaking his name.

Pandemic: Incidents of Mortality
James Niven, 1918 (Medical Officer of Health)

They dropped on their desks, locked into times tables,
their histories and grammar, dropped in the face of their futures,
they dropped at lineshafts and lathes, dropped boring

an engine block, rifling a barrel, they dropped in the street,
dropped from trams, they dropped in their dreams,
from hand to mouth they dropped, dropped to their deaths

from fireside rugs, they dropped queuing for mackerel,
lentils and milk, tripped on a breath and dropped, they dropped
at their leisure, mid-sing-along, on the laugh of a music-hall joke,

they dropped at Armstrong & Whitworths, at Crossley's,
at Shell, they dropped in the bath between an idea and its germ,
they kissed and they dropped, dropped even as sperm

cracked egg, when pulling a pint they dropped, dropped
at the mop, the infirmary sluice, before matron they dropped
and she dropped too, they dropped in Ancoats, in Gorton

they dropped, dropped in Bramhall, in Wilmslow they dropped,
they dropped on the platform as the troops limped home,
dropped between the envelope and the telegram's stone.

Man Engine
1919, Levant Mine, Cornwall

Not a mechanical cutter turning out
workers, ready-made husbands and fathers,
but a gothic invention to keep them

to time, and raising them again
from their dark houses, from sollor to step,
a clockwork tree winding back

to the blues and greens, the red froth
on a wild sea. A two-step, dancing pillar
of men fetched up at the face – the shift's

long incubation – in tin rooms and hallways.
Here's how the fall happens: iron strap,
engine rod, gear, and the women begin –

not dressed for their newly pressed status
as yet – their longest years.

The English Translation

If God spare my life, ere many yeares I wyl cause a boy that driveth the plough to know more of the Scripture, than he doust.
    – William Tyndale

Ploughboy, –
                    I give you words as bread
For you to hold on your own tongue that you might
Know the taste of God, that you might read
For yourself that which was done for you by Him
And in your name. I write myself a heretic,
Inter my soul under all the *bedlam-mad* of Rome.
On each furrowed line, I sow the scriptures
With good seed, return them to an honest earth.

I will birth this text so unlike its ruined-self
You would not make them out for kin. From
Exile and before I burn, I will sail this grain
Across the channel for you to raise in faith,
In grace, slipped into the sheaves of common
Books, in bales of wool, in casks of wine.

Treasure

> *Let them be known to one and other*
> – Margaret Larney, Newgate Prison, 1758

Sir, –
With this last breath of mine,
I plead my belly, send to you
my second son that I have coined.

Wrought from me, the muck
and treason I have milled,
he is a golden mote flung mid-
explosion through a widening sky.

Give him sight of his brother,
that other star that I have made.
Let my twin suns burnish the day,
let them be brighter by my night.

Sir, I am smelt. To you I send my trove;
my finest work; my sovereign boy.

Lookout

I meant to write about death, only life came breaking in as usual
— Virginia Woolf

Others have climbed this ringlet of steps
to good weather, but when I come
it's after a night squall. In the wreckage
of rain salt seeps from the frame.

In the path of the sea seagulls are laughing.
The tide runs ragged on the beach,
waves batter the shore as a ship
battles north: Conrad would've made

something of this. From a mirror foxed
as the walls, my mottled self is watching.
We all have our towers. But here on an
up-draught there is only the tom-foolery

of flight. I'm a wishbone in sight of its wish.
The seagulls are laughing and flying stock still.

Notes

Drowning
Mcalister's boy is a character in *To the Lighthouse*.

The Light Fantastic
'Be Still My Soul' is sung to the slow movement in *Finlandia*.

The Mile Road at Midnight
Boddies is the Manchester beer Boddingtons.

Honeymoons
British High Commissioner, Sir Percy Cox, in 1922, created the border between Iraq, Kuwait and Nejd (Saudi Arabia).

Coattails
In 1910 the discovery that cyanogen (a deadly poison) was present in Haley's Comet brought widespread panic since the earth's trajectory would take it directly through the tail.

Residency
Emily Wilding Davison hid in the Chapel of St Mary Undercroft to have her place of residency recorded as the Palace of Westminster.

Crossings
Ned Parfett died on 29 October 1918 at Valenciennes as he was collecting clothes from the quartermaster before returning to England on two weeks leave.

The Left-Handed Bride
Morganatic marriages between unequal ranks prevented titles being passed on to wives and offspring. Known also as left-handed marriages because the groom held his bride's right hand in his left.

Requiem from the steps of Pendlebury Station
Anna Akhmatova's poem Requiem carried a forward telling of queues on the prison lines. Asked "Can you describe this?" she said, "Yes, I can."

Pandemic: Incidents of Mortality
Details are taken from the *Annual Report for 1918*, of the Medical Officer of Health for Manchester.

Man Engine
The man-engine at the Levant tin mine in Cornwall was full of men during a shift-change when it collapsed crushing 31 miners.

Treasure
Convicted of high treason for filing coins of the realm Margaret Larney was sentenced to be burned at the stake. Pregnant at the time, her sentence was postponed but not commuted.